To Thais Reynolds,
one of God's little lambs

Copyright © 1992 by Patricia Richardson Mattozzi
All rights reserved
First published in 1992 by Derrydale Books
distributed by Outlet Book Company, Inc.,
a Random House Company,
40 Engelhard Avenue
Avenel, New Jersey 07001

Manufactured in the United States

Designed by Melissa Ring

Library of Congress Cataloging-in-Publication Data
Mattozzi, Patricia.
My shepherd is the Lord / by Patricia Richardson Mattozzi.
p.   cm.
Summary: Watercolor paintings accompany the text of the
twenty-third psalm.
ISBN 0-517-08145-8
1. Bible.   O.T.   Psalms XXIII—Juvenile literature.   [1. Bible.
O.T.   Psalms XXIII.]   I. Title.
BS1450   23rd.M328   1992   92-12768
223'.209505—dc20   CIP
AC

8   7   6   5   4   3   2   1

He cares for me so tenderly,
my needs are satisfied.

The Lord is my shepherd,
forever by my side.

My Shepherd is the Lord

Patricia Richardson Mattozzi

Derrydale Books
New York • Avenel, New Jersey

He has me lie among the hills
in pastures green and sweet.
There I lie in safety—
a faithful watch He keeps.

He leads me to a quiet place
by waters cool and still.
His peace and love enfold me,
I seek to do His will.

He frees my heart of sadness,
    loneliness, and grief—
His gentle touch brings wholeness,
    healing, and relief.

He teaches me to love
in my words and in my deeds,

Doing what is right and good—
helping those in need.

With those who seek to harm me,
    He shows me how to live,
Always full of mercy,
    ready to forgive.

He seals me with His spirit,
blessings overflow.
In paths of love and goodness
I will surely go.

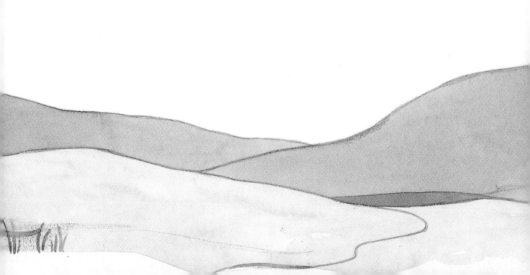

When darkness comes and shadows fall
His staff becomes my guide.
I will fear no evil—
the Lord is by my side.

A special place of glory
awaits me at the end.

There I'll live forever
with Jesus, my best friend!